Slow

Skinny

Sad

High

Low

I'm up here, honked the goose
Down below to the moose.

Compared with the small chigger
The mouse is much bigger.

The Wacky World of OPPOSITES

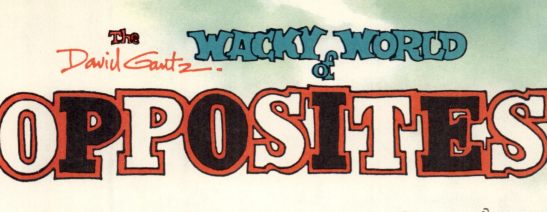

A pretty cardinal said, "Good day."
Two ugly vultures replied, "Go away!"

A large pig in a silly wig,
   Said to a small toad doing a jig:
"You're terribly tiny—I'm awfully big."

Top · Bottom

Here's the circus family Michael,
Riding on their unicycle.
There's old Pop
Juggling on top
And brother Tom's got 'em
Sitting on the bottom.

Truth·Lie

"Did the stork bring me, Granny Ruth?"
"Jimmy dear, I must tell the truth.
 I simply can't tell you a lie.
 You didn't just drop in from the sky."

Above · Below

Adrift above the sea, deep and dark
Below, a hungry, hungry shark

Dark·Light

Hey you, in that dark, dank, dingy cave,
The one they call Ol' Kinky Dave,
C'm out here in the sparkly, bright light,
And be rid of that dark, dank, dingy night.

Quiet · Loud

Quiet Kenneth Quenton
Asked Mr. Benton
For a long-expected raise.
Loud Boss Benton
Said, "NO!" to Quenton,
Leaving him in a dizzy daze.

Big · Little

When Tammy Tittle was barely two
She got a puppy as little as her shoe.
When Tammy Tittle was almost three
The pup was much bigger than she.

Friend·Foe

A lion, a hare, a fox, and a bear
All became fast friends.
Along came a crow
With nasty thoughts to sow,
And every friend became a foe.

Fast·Slow

Bragged rapid Ron Rabbit,
"I've got a bad habit—
I'm first because I'm fast."
Said Myrtle the turtle,
"I know that I'm slow,
But I am not always last."

Float · Sink

Hilda Hippo, in a pretty pink bow,
Launched her boat for a midday row.
Her chubby friend was at her side
Elton Elephant came for the ride.
But never did the sailors think
That Hilda's boat would sink…and sink!
"If we can't float," said she to him,
"Then shall we take a midday swim?"

Heavy·Light

Ron threw a heavy rock
In the water from the dock.
Willy watched a light leaf float
As he rowed by in his boat.

Asleep • Awake

Two sailors, wide awake and quaking like jelly,
Shipwrecked on a sleeping whale's belly.

In · Out

Mice making merry without a single care
In and out of the mouth of a snoring bear.

Wise·Foolish

Foolish Mike McTavish climbed up a mountain
To see his friend, wise Wilfred Fountain.
Mike asked, "What's the secret of life?"
"The secret," said Wilfred,
"Is to be free of strife."

Slim·Stout

Jim Quinn is rather slim
Everyone thinks the world of him.
His brother Tim is very stout
And a lazy good-for-nothing lout.

Young·Old

Early every morning
When the sun comes up
Young Ben goes walking
With his old grandpop.

Black·White

Penguins make such a handsome sight
All dressed up in their black and white.

Good·Evil

Godfrey Gragon
Beat the evil dragon.
But when the dragon began to weep
Good Godfrey gave him a flower to keep.

Deep · Shallow

"My," said the giraffe,
"This lake is shallow."
"It's deep," said the bear,
"With ample room to wallow."

Here·There

"Why are we here?"
Asked mountaineer Van Der Vere.
"Because nothing's up there!"
Replied climber O'Hare.

Meek·Fierce

A meek little lamb
Strayed from her meadow
And met up with a bull,
A fierce sort of fellow.

None · Many

Hey nonny, nonny, no-nose Nooney
Coming down the lane looking looney.
"Where's your nose?" I ask in jest.
"I've got none," he says, "just let it rest."
"Nooney," I say, "meet three-nose Benny.
He was born with two too many."

Huge · Tiny

Kafka, a huge and horrible bug,
Put the tiny tick in a water jug.

Polite · Rude

Polite Molly Mankew
Would always say thank you.

Rude Rod Rugetto
Would just as soon forget to.

Beginning·End

Smedley Snake wasn't too bright,
For sometimes in the dark of night,
When his end would come in sight,
He'd give himself a painful bite.

Tall

Short

Fast

Fat

Happy